pe

peep

DANIELLE BLAU

WAYWISER

First published in 2022 by

THE WAYWISER PRESS

Christmas Cottage, Church Enstone, Chipping Norton, Oxfordshire, OX7 4NN, UK
P.O. Box 6205, Baltimore, MD 21206, USA
https://waywiser-press.com

9 7 5 3 1 2 4 6 8

A CIP catalogue record for this book is available from the British Library.

ISBN 978-1-911379-03-4

MIX
Paper from
responsible sources
FSC® C013056

Printed and bound by
T. J. Books Ltd., Padstow, Cornwall, PL28 8RW

For Kai, my home address

Acknowledgments

Grateful acknowledgment is made to the publications in which the following poems, sometimes in quite different forms, first appeared:

Australian Book Review: "The Vernal Equinox Story"

The Baffler: "How Long Now Since the Mailman's Gone Missing?"

The Harvard Review online: "Formal Proof That the Universe Is Neither Cruel nor Kind, and That This Is the Greatest Conceivable Horror"

The Literary Review: "No News Today," "The Insider," and "N^{th} Sunday in Ordinary Time"

Narrative: "Conversations with Death," "Villanelle," "A Suicide Bomber (Eighteen Seconds to Go) Foresees Her Death" [as "The Suicide Bomber's Song, Minutes Before"], "Arpeggio Progression in Missing Key," "Full Rhymes to Live (More Fully) By," "Inventory," and "The Spare Room"

The Paris Review: "I Am the Perennial Head of This One-person Subcutaneous Wrecking Crew"

Ploughshares: "Penance"

Plume Anthology of Poetry 5: "magus"

Plume Anthology of Poetry 6: "In the Valley of the Choice Vine II: The Wax Museum"

Plume Anthology of Poetry 8: "Whose Hands"

Plume Poetry: "Hapax Legomenon," "Creation Myth," and "The gap between"

Saint Ann's Review: "The Fear"

Unsaid: "Some Views f/ Thingèd Surface"

I also want to offer a special thanks to the Poetry Society of America for publishing a number of these poems in a chapbook, *mere eye*, and to D.A. Powell for selecting that chapbook and writing its introduction.

Acknowledgments

Deepest gratitude to Phil Hoy, Joe Harrison, and everyone at Waywiser Press. I am forever indebted to Vijay Seshadri.

Thank you, thank you—last but certainly not least—to Eve Attermann, Derrick Belcham, Josh Bell, Tina Bennett, Emily Fragos, Rebecca Newberger Goldstein, Yael Goldstein-Love, Nicholas Hiltner, Tim Hobbs, Yusef Komunyakaa, Smriti Mallapaty, Meg Metzger, David McLendon, Robert Ostrom, Jasmine Pisapia, Matthew Rohrer, Brenda Shaughnessy, and Michael Wiegers.

Contents

Foreword by Vijay Seshadri

The first impressions Danielle Blau's poems give the reader are impressions of newness and immediacy. These impressions also happen to be, along with the many others that billow out of these rich and abundant poems, the second and fifth (and fiftieth) impressions. Blau's newness and immediacy aren't ephemeral or fugitive. They aren't calculated or contrived. And they aren't generated from fashionable detailing or cultural signalling. Her poems glitter, and they're incredibly energetic, but they're never flashy, and their persuasiveness derives from deep sources. Though her flexible diction is present-day, though she has a gender-specific savviness and élan that probably wouldn't have been possible before the advent of the twenty-first century (or thereabouts), though she's street-wise, nothing in her work is just contemporary, nothing is independent of anything else. As hip as she is, she's also a throwback to the Romantic vocation of organic form. All her effects are emanations of the fullness with which her sensibility inhabits language and the confident way her imagination takes possession of her experience.

These poems command their existential and historical moment, but they also radiate inward and outward from it. Here is the first stanza of the introductory poem, "The Vernal Equinox Story," which serves as a creation myth for the book:

On the twentieth of March, day & night
hung in the balance, & we
would chant our palindromes—*Redder. Peep. Noon. Oh who was*
it I saw. Oh who
—would fold
into ash
tree shadows, till cloven
sky quivered, aswarm, & Light
spake again: Behold,
                    my Forms.

This is a flawless blend of surprise and inevitability. The "swarming"—the trundled, precarious rhythms and cliffhanging lineations, the loops, the typographic ornamentation, the syntactic inversions, the archaisms—powerfully suggests a writer conscious of and susceptible to, in a time when everything is available to our fingertips, the densities of the Information Age. The fact that the stanza's ultimate destination turns out to be in the vicinity of the Book of Genesis suggests a writer who not only knows instinctively what to do with these susceptibilities, seductions, and enthusiasms, who not only knows how to free herself from her circumstances, but, besides, has a judicious control of some serious ambition. The fact that the stanza arrives at a magical metrical resolution in the last lines suggests a writer with a terrific ear.

Blau is generally addicted to word play, though her addiction is disciplined and redemptively entrepreneurial. Palindromes have a particular fetishistic appeal for her, for example, but space doesn't allow for more than a gloss of the many ways in which she transforms this predilection into poetic advantages and opportunities. She has her simple fun with palindromes, yes, but palindromes also, as mirrors and mirrorings, become principles of both organization and meaning. Reversals, dialectical oppositions, doublings—all are milked for compositional strategies, psychological insights, and metaphysics. They provide Blau with endless opportunities to multiply significance and maintain compositional coherence as a counterweight to her restless, acquisitive, headstrong imagination. In a poem such as "Full Rhymes to Live (More Fully) By," one of Blau's all-over-painting-type poems, rhyme (a kind of aural mirroring) is turned inside out in such a way as to look to the past while anticipating the future, which is something that is done with regularity in these poems.

The allegiances are contemporary. The dominant sensibility is baroque. Blau likes to complicate things, confident as she is that her gift for drama and her narrative verve can get her out of any situation she finds herself in. But she's just as capable of honoring the old imperatives and handling the simpler, more ancient tools of poetry and rhetoric, and capable of doing so with unstrained facility. Her irony, for example, can be complex, rueful, tender, beautifully modulated, liberating in its sympathy:

I've been taking Italian classes, so I could probably understand what it says on Vincenza Benanti's grave in Calvary Cemetery, a 20-minute ride from my home by bus, or on Maria Lauletti's grave in the Evergreens Cemetery, 15 minutes by bike.

This is from "We're Human, All of Us Girls, and We're Young," a poem commemorating the hundred-and-eighth anniversary, in 2019, of the Triangle Shirtwaist Factory fire, in Greenwich Village—New York City's deadliest industrial disaster, which killed a hundred and forty-six garment workers, a hundred and twenty-three of whom were women.

She can also, along with this kind of empathy, and along with delight in her energy, exercise a pure, still, and mysterious lyricism. This is the entirety of "Whose Hands":

Strange way for life, as known it, to end.
The old world like tenants
making off in the night without notice
without even a scribbled napkin
slipped under my door.

Had brunch today with H.
–What is this? Radicchio?
–No. I think it's just cabbage.
Later, went and knocked
upstairs. Their rent was overdue.

No answer.
Dark through the lintel.
Whose hands are these?

Whose hair?
Inside, it seemed, a woman laughing.

peep is a tour de force, and it's more than a tour de force. It displays deep within itself, for all its intellectual and imaginative power and self-delight, a curious tenderness and vulnerability. The book glories in language and thinking; it's imaginative and bold; but it's also intimate. If I were asked to account for this intimacy, especially in the face of all the other effects that Blau realizes, I might say, diffidently, that Blau is the performer of her own experience, but she is also its scholar and critic. The doubling of consciousness, like the mirroring of the palindrome, creates an in-between space, a dimple in reality that allows something else, some other embodiment of meaning, to arrive and situate itself. What that other thing, that third thing, is is an object that invites and accommodates endless contemplation and reflection.

Are we not drawn onward, we few, drawn onward to new era

—a palindrome

The Vernal Equinox Story

On the twentieth of March, day & night
hung in the balance, & we
would chant our palindromes—*Redder. Peep. Noon. Oh who was*
it I saw. Oh who
—would fold
into ash
tree shadows, till cloven
sky quivered, aswarm, & Light
spake again: Behold,
                my Forms.

Then came a reckoning
for us, the indefinite—for the smoke-
skinned &
vapornatured—for the reedy—for
the roily of temper, roily
of hue—as Sun, uncaging

coiled ribs, exhaled pure
vitriolage of Spring
&—once more
newly heaven-
bent on ravishment, & scour, & scraping
clean without

distinction—down-
lusted blind translucence towards us,
who clutched
the wasting
dusk cast
by burnished junipers—*we few*—for

splendid pestilence, sad
match, we burnt &
lumpish dust—who cherished the stalk, begetter
of shade—who picked our first-
borns' names from
the thousand words for gray—who hymned to

without form & void, Oh Void
& formless Void—while all
around, the spindlebushes, Winter's
shrinking nuns, by red-
blooded enormity were drawn, drawn to the brink, drawn on
to shrieking

bloom—as there
beneath, the crouched
in prayer—the blasted, the dazzleworn—
scorched wheat in wind were
our skirling limbs, who
sing: But—but it's
us—we few out here—here—here—us now
still—we silt—we here—we water & sand—we muck—we filth—we
Matter. Yes. Behold,
                our Forms.

I

The Fear

1

If you're like
me, a person

who's alive
today

in this world even

now as we speak there's
no more I can say.

2

What causes it?
No one knows.

3

What causes it? No one

knows. It
is still much too early. No
comment.

4

But whether we know all
the answers yet, or we
don't doesn't

matter. What
we need is to stop

take a look
inside and face—

yes, face—the issue head-
on. We are making progress
just by talking we're doing

good work, we are
getting closer. Thank you. This
is the most important conversation

we ever could have.

5

What causes it?

Gluten.

6

Diagnosis: angina due to
probable excess
of aspartame;

subclinical (incipient)
aphasia; a face
at the bottom

of a plash of black
water at
the bottom of a

black bathroom sink
Prognosis: get out get out get
out get out get out get out get out

7

You know that Thai spot in Soho where
the bathroom walls are one-way
mirrors? Peep, it's called. I think it's

closed now. But their eel tacos were good, and in the bathroom, on all four sides
you saw people eat
dinner with red

faces that flickered in and
out like
pinched little flames. It was

the zeros or the
aughts or however you're supposed to call it, so mood lighting etc, and you could
see them but

they couldn't see you, you could see them but they
couldn't see you, you could see them but they couldn't see
you, get out get out get out get out get out get

8

I remember though
once I
was afraid

of something
like at
school Ms.

Boom
the gym teacher
or someone calling

me dimple-
witted
my mother

opened her
hand and
there were three

fern seeds
fern seeds
make good children

turn invisible
she said
just carry a

seed in your
pocket and
pop it next

time that
you feel
scared just one

two three
poof
you are gone

out
get out get
out get out

get out and
when she
finally did

I hurled her
stupid seeds
across

my room
and stomped and
stomped and

stamped them out
under my heel
they were

so pathetic
smashed
up all watery

they weren't even
anything
just some Green

Giant sweet
peas
from the can

9

No but what was I saying again
about that Thai restaurant we all
used to love? So there I

was and dead
of November by the way and I was having the Mighty
Khan Stir Fry, and Frieda ordered—I can't

remember—but we were
talking about what
had happened and she was like No

way in hell, because—so you guys know
who Vladimir Petru is? Oh. Well anyway,
well actually never mind.

10

Although if you're like me—Are
you like me? Please like me. You

have seen me
on my page

of the book, you've
seen my face and it is good

to see
my face in the Good Book you've read

my name you know my
face you've seen me scattered on the face

of the waters and it is good it
is good it is good it is

good it's good, isn't it?
Good. Then

right this way, Madam. Please, follow
me. Follow me. I'm right

here, I'm that
dot over there on your screen.

No, over there.

11

But there's another me
inside of me

and she is wearing Hedi Slimane. Wait—
how? Does she have

rich parents? No clue.
See? There's

a lot about me
we don't know. It's like I've read

about what makes
for best quality living-

room furniture: you cannot tell
by outward

look of the upholstery alone,
which, case in point, you

know, the me
inside, she truly

might surprise you: her skirt is short
like really

short and sorry

not so
age appropriate. Fuck. Don't look now but

look: the poor thing, I think
she thinks she's

working it. She's like Oops, is
my epidermis

trending? Christ. People like that
scare me. To each

his own, I mean, but personally
I'm more the down-

home type, I guess. Me, I'll just go in this
fyi, borrowed
likeness of shrunk death.

12

My mother used to sing me
this song before bed

about a sweet little doll dear

who is the most beautiful
thing in the world

but then she gets lost
in like a field or large meadow. My beautiful

mother's hair smells like trimmed hedges
and the kind of off-

brand loose cigarettes she
gets from the Chinese

discount if it's late and all the regular
stores are closed and she sits very

very close and tucks me in so
tight it

hurts but I really
don't mind and when she's done

singing she
leans in for a kiss and I see

there's a hole in her face where
her face should be. And her

arms trotted off by the dogs dear.

13

Yesterday I ate yuzu fruit and spat
the seeds across the room from
where I sat in the chair. It wasn't

the worst. I meant
to get clementines. I count all my
seeds after dark. My chair is a Casket.

No,
it's a Gasket. A Gasca. It's the White
Grub-Suckling Chaise by Jesùs Gasca.

14

I saw my face once
after sundown
in a hole in the sidewalk that

had filled all the way
up with rain. Inside my face
was a hole the color of

fall sky after a storm, and inside
the hole was a glow-in-the-
dark red sign

with some white
that said KFC. Gross. It's—
just think about it. I mean, it

isn't even real.

15

Does anybody know
something good to do with 15 lbs of yuzu fruit?
Just now

I wrote that. Did
you see? That
was me

just writing that just now.

16

I was in
third
grade when they

gave me a
prize for
some

poem I'd mostly
plagiarized off
some

big dead
guy and
my mother was

so proud she
took
me out for

Olive Garden
gross
what a tacky

The Fear

bitch so skip
to the good
part

later on
in
the parking lot

I found a
hole
that had a

mirror in it
and that
mirror

looked in at
a mirror
in

me that
had a
hole in it

A Suicide Bomber (Eighteen Seconds to Go) Foresees Her Death

In the place above
the place we are now

a soap vendor
bows at the waist

a pale brick drops
in a child's left palm

the tote in his right
spilling grain

a goose egg
hidden in rags goes

unpaid for (*Poor half-*
wit, they cast their eyes down)

a window crack isn't
yet noticed

by the silhouette
perched on the sill

a girl's sudden
round cheeks—

exactly like here
but, up there, when you

prick them they bleed.

The Insider

I am baking a cake, want to help? OK but it's important to be careful: measure well. An inchworm once cast a shadow blotting out my birthday. Everything is smaller than itself down here.

The gap between

the platform &
the train meant

certain death
Granma said. Not this time,

no, of course & maybe
also not the next

but one of these trips to see her only
daughter's family, soon & then

won't you feel like monsters?
Mom took her suitcase, we nodded

yes. With Gran in town, it was
no swearing allowed, no

boys, seesaws, and loud voices
were reserved for her daily sacred shrill

devotions to panic
& rage, should she

find me playing tightrope-
walker on the curb, or petting a too

large dog, or letting my face
go under water

at our nextdoor neighbors' pool. Still
we managed to smile & tiptoe

for however long it took (except once
after she chased me through the garden

with a spatula, Dad said
pack up now, get out)—

The gap between

or else we'd whisper in the upstairs den
until the sighing died

down in the kitchen, which meant
she'd finally fallen asleep. But all together

on a round flowered rug
we'd sit & sing "Once had a

sweet little doll dear" on rare visits
to Granma's apartment, or so

at least I always did think—& yet last
week when we went there to divvy her

things: her home, I hardly
knew the place, must've been

years & the carpets ran
wall to wall. Beside the bed

was a pink jaw-shaped box
& I remembered how she

never would lock
the bathroom door, how

I learned about dentures one
morning & how awful

her fledgling gums, caught,
prayerful eyes—ghoulish—how small

she was without teeth. & it might
well have been seismic—

the chasm
till Track Number Seven—

The gap between

from where she pressed
her bag tight &

considered her exit:
it often distorts how depth

& distance are felt—an astro-
cytoma—though we'd

never heard of
such a thing

back then, or of her favorite
sister, Lilibet, who drowned

when they were both girls (in the belly
of that ratty bench, Gran's original pieces

for piano, all titled
To Lil). & we're still not sure

if she ever composed the famous
plaint to Amtrak (if so, it passed

unanswered: she would no doubt
have saved their reply)—or in the cupboard

why a chipped
saucer was kept wrapped in linen

alone on a shelf—
or what chinks,

distantly, in her night-
table drawer if you pull at

its porcelain knob; that tiny key must
have vanished, I swear, we looked

everywhere. We tried.

II

II

Ostinato

I've missed you
as a woman misses the last words
of a poorly dubbed film

everyone used to love.
Listen: she'll
play through the start of the end

credit song, and then she'll press
rewind, still
all night, still, all night.

Full Rhymes to Live (More Fully) By

1

Do you dream
in turtle green?

Then, when you wake
try
washing well…

By suppertime, there's not a trace
of soft &
dying in its shell.

2

One day (it's bound to happen) they
will put you on hold & when

they do, I mean it, listen
really *listen* to the music. Have you heard "Whiter Shade

of Pale" by Michael Bolton straight
through? Carly Simon's "Itsy Bitsy Spider" will come

as a surprise to you, probably, too. You can sit

all afternoon with your chipped

saucer, cracked mug, under
your sick potted jade—have everything

fade except wood-
wind synth & the sense that you're first, now

in line. No really, it's fine. It's OK. See? Just like how
one day will come full,

heady raps at your door

that, like me, you'll

never answer.

3

One day, there's a chance
you may
find yourself

at a party: Don't be caught

without fresh
little candies or something, it's polite
to bring snacks, melon, wine,

& remember that people
like questions
aimed at themselves regarding

themselves, also cookies
are, as a rule, received
well by groups—

a kind I like's called Famous
Amos.

If (at some point) you find
they've been calling you by

some other asshole's name, you may
feel angry. This will fade.

Catch your breath
down in the study or large
closet with the brooms
—You'll be surprised by the coatroom

how it's hardly

just for coats: There are boots
in there & too-

high heels

stockings, even

sometimes. Sweaters.

The goodbye can get hard, so
better to keep it brief.
Should they lean in, don't

look at their mouth:

Aim straight for their cheek
& if you really are
lucky, now

you're close to faded home

you'll find your clothes are   not your own.

4

The best time to ride your bike

is at night   when

your hedge shears are broken,

your grass shears

are broken. In the place where
you stack folded laundry, there's an

Full Rhymes to Live (More Fully) By

ash silhouette of laundry. The old shed you
stash your lawn tools in

burned down in '92.

Yes, a nighttime bike
ride's your best bet: All you've spent

your days breaking

past the blindcurving lake   you

forget

now   you're ash silhouette.

5

Has it

ever occurred to you, you're

all alone?

Shit

motherfucker

it should have, long ago.

6

The greatest fables of them all
are about us, how we're varying shades of small.

You know the one about
when I found

a jade spider at the foot
of our shade tree? You should.

It was dark, it was time
for the game show. My mother was crying.

Inventory

she was making soup from
cast-off dress shirts she found
in the bedding when she
realized he was gone

and for years judging by
his style of sleeve (nobody
wore snap buttons these days)
but often hunger they say
is thirst wrongly felt maybe
loneness in concentrate
tastes like being
mostly content

possible too that she was
a turnip had forsworn blood
and sinew for one flawless
white sigh

she stirred and wondered
what (if anything) was hers
while the kitchen bloomed a
slanting that belonged to
afternoon where just out-
side the window a vole was
pulling up vegetables

a yam breathed to the
glistening tooth I love
you come here let's go
home

Creation Myth

We never expected this. Shapes
in our shapeless garden. The crude

mound we've been growing, Dirt,
is gone. One of the shapes points

to itself, "Willem," or no,
"Phyllis," it's hard to understand.

"That thing," you say, "I think that
thing's Dirt mixed with far whispers."

Low chants from the rubbish shed.
In every direction obscenely

figs sprout. "I'm going in," you yawn,
and of course Pop's too busy with

his slime-mold farm to come out
and see. Meanwhile, terrible groans

are general. Terrible wailing and
gnashing and multiplying.

You stroll by, "Dirt's back," snap
your chewing gum like a yo-yo, "well,

I mean, not him exactly but a slew
of Baby Dirts." I turn. The shape

called Willem is there and, behind it,
our garden, a plot of suckling mounds.

On my cheek I can
feel the shape's spiny breath.

Gravel tears in its eyes—
my eyes, it's then I notice.

Whose Hands

Strange way for life, as known it, to end.
The old world like tenants
making off in the night without notice
without even a scribbled napkin
slipped under my door.

Had brunch today with H.
–What is this? Radicchio?
–No. I think it's just cabbage.
Later, went and knocked
upstairs. Their rent was overdue.

No answer.
Dark through the lintel.
Whose hands are these?

Whose hair?
Inside, it seemed, a woman laughing.

The Spare Room

I have done things I know
can't be

undone. Or that's far
too strong; swap

out *know* for
it seems—or, better: forget the old

drip, Memory
who (swollen

gams, asthma) falls
forever behind, humming

pestilential static she
insists on calling *our*

sweet childhood ditties. And look
what a mess she's made

of her slacks, rounding
the bend (at last) just as

a Buick sloshes by: not bad
luck, no, she means

to do it, no, no, she lives for leaving
muckprints of her

own ticking
hooves! Still—

it's sad (if I'm honest)
how years have hewn

from Memory a monster
since (I swear) once I would

The Spare Room

let the poor girl come
to me, even in bed. *It's filled*

with biting
midges and rain and our name

snaking loud behind glass
windows all through the whole house and

out to a thunder on the porch saying You been
making messes

and getting into bad
things *and hard grown-*

up feet hard hard hard down
the stairs to the grass getting closer—

the broken tree-swing
where you chain me, she lies: what, at

dusk, I tuck
Memory into is nothing

but a tire, grown
pillow-soft beneath its layers

of blankety sedge—livable terms for
us both, till she went and learned to

slither loose somehow. My
predawn hunt today has

left me upended
kitchen table and chairs, a fissuring

television, screendoor skewed half
off its hinges, sugar bowl

in shards, yet Memory
seemingly nowhere; still

(and still) from
some near place: her crackling crooning *time*

to spare now baby come
come there's room this

room's dark well
we know it

how sweet how close we
are both and how dark

the dark's welling yes how
well we both do know this room's close dark but far

far from empty.

Villanelle

There is an order. Such an order.
Each event a word that must be read
or else, my friend—Today I woke up shorter,

sleep playing pestle to my twin bed's mortar,
me the poor shaved meat. But no regret—
an order to these things, you see, there's order.

Each man a crack at playing cosmic sorter.
Within each uncracked code-shell is a threat.
Today, take notice; time is getting shorter.

Two speckled eggs. Omens from the Lord, or
Nature, the clouds, some darker silhouette.
Listen, my friend: what they say's an order.

And at this moment's close, you'll cross the border
into the moment after—seems no end
of days lived longly but they're short and shorter

at each turn, the world speaks: I record her
though she only talks in languages long dead,
there is an order—yes—an awful order
my friend, wake up! Your shadow's growing shorter.

Hapax Legomenon

Literally "thing said once," hapax legomenon *refers to a word that appears in a text on only one occasion. When the text is an ancient one in a dead language, hapax legomena create difficulties in decipherment, since inferring the meaning of a given word from its context becomes increasingly uncertain the fewer examples of the word there are in existence.*

She said, *Last night really*
was hapax legomenon, which I

nodding, took
(with the ricocheted

door, plus the draft let in)
to mean: bound to

not happen again.

                                                Well, more

than enough

on my

plate, thank you, without her & her
outlandish diction, what

with this toilsome coupling
of referents & names: every

day, I swear, worse than
the last & every last

day worse than Tolstoy. Say, why
not call

the lot of us Anna
Alexandrovna Ivanovna Stetlovna & go

whole hog, hmm? Who
could have told much

difference, given
how unrelenting the present

demand for
marginalia is

on a man
wishing simply

to follow
the gist! Yet no matter where

he turns: things
sloughing off their

terms; signs freshly
threshed from

the chaff of events—oh, did it ever get
more

cut &
dried each

passing year I
lived: this world's

a wicked wheat field.

But what

about her: good as her

word? Ha! Hardly
could leave

well
enough

alone, it seems, dear
thing. As a Kurdish boy (gently

sprouting acne, touchingly
bent on calling me

Sir) she'd often come
to read

my meter
& then—that one

April (glistening, brief)

—a hurt starling, she
made her

home
below my eaves deep in my walls I felt her walk I felt her limp her listing

lovelorn pulse

—not to mention

Hapax Legomenon

the guy (I'm all but certain)

at the market last week who sold me

sturgeon; she said, *Since*

prehistoric age unchanged—

which, nodding, I took to mean: this fish

is eaten poached

or braised.

We're Human, All of Us Girls, and We're Young

(Sunday, March 25, 2019/the 108th Anniversary of the Triangle Shirtwaist Factory Fire)

Rosie Freedman (18, asphyxiation/burns) was eventually identified by her uncle, Isaac Hine, but she was originally listed as Annie Colletti (30, burns), and Annie Colletti was originally mistaken for her, though identified correctly by her mother, Rose, on March 28, 1911. I wonder if they knew each other.

I live in a Queens neighborhood that is cupped by cemeteries, but I used to live on Hicks St (Brooklyn) between Kane and Degraw, a three-minute walk from 81 Degraw, which is where Francesca Caputo (16 or 17, multiple injuries, name also given as Frances Capatta/Cabutto/Capotto) lived, until identified by Salvatore Natone (relationship unknown).

The Brooklyn-Queens Expressway was built in 1936. It runs as an underpass along Hicks and cleaves the street in half. To walk to 81 Degraw, I would cross the BQE using the bridge at Degraw.

Anna Altman (15 or 16, fractured skull) was born in Narewka, Russia (now Podlaskie, Poland) circa 1895 and immigrated to the United States, to New York, probably with her mother and multiple sisters, circa 1906, which meant she was here for something close to five years before jumping from a window of the factory's ninth floor.

Lizzie Adler (24, multiple injuries) was born in Bucharest in 1887 and came to the US three months before the fire. At some point her father and mother probably called her *bebelus meu*, I can say this because someone I knew once, a deejay named Dru, spent most of his adult life in Romania, until, forced to leave for reasons I have never understood, he moved to New York, where he and I were briefly very close. I'm not sure where Dru is now, maybe here, but on my own it's not as easy telling myself from the sprawl of an unlit room.

I was born at a different point in time than Francesca Caputo. Probably we still wouldn't know each other. Back then, on Hicks St, I knew hardly any of my neighbors.

The girls who were too burnt were identified by buttons on their cuffs, heels on their shoes, darns in their stockings, braids in their hair, caps on their teeth. It's hard to tell, sometimes, which facts matter.

Once I took a bath with my goldfish. I was with Miri Listokin, my best friend at the time. We were very young, she must not have understood, she must not have known air suffocates fish. I can see her cupped hands, still, the frantic pink gills.

Sarah Brodsky (21, asphyxiation/burns) was identified by her cousin, Morris, and by Isidor Brozolsky, a man who called himself her sweetheart, and who recognized the body by a ring he had given her.

Some dentist, probably a quack, told me the gaps between my teeth were bad, that one day, looking down at an apple, there they'd be, because it's hard for teeth on their own. Now my real teeth are inside of bigger, tooth-colored shells, but a handful of people know that. I wonder if you could tell.

I was 19 or 20 when I shared a one-bedroom on Hicks with my cat, Francesca. Dave Magee and I had just broken up. There was a shaman Dave believed in. A past illness. A dead fiancée named Vanessa. I told people I didn't mind living over the BQE, it was the closest I'd come to oceanfront property I said, but it sounded more like a seashell than the sea, and me the small meat in a spiraling conch.

I've been taking Italian classes, so I could probably understand what it says on Vincenza Benanti's grave in Calvary Cemetery, a 20-minute ride from my home by bus, or on Maria Lauletti's grave in the Evergreens Cemetery, 15 minutes by bike.

"We like new hats as well as any other young women," said 23-year-old Clara Lemlich in Yiddish to a crowd of fellow garment workers, November, 1909. "We're human, all of us girls, and we're young." Her speech spiraled into a large-scale strike, and the strike led many factories to bow to workers' demands, functional fire escapes, for example, and unlocked doors. The Triangle Shirtwaist was not one of those factories.

Three months ago I went to Vienna with my best friend. We stayed with her aunt and uncle, who kept calling me the same wrong name. They were sad to see us leave. They said, "Please do come again one day to visit us, Fabienne." And I promised I would.

Some Views f/ Thingèd Surface

[View No. One]

She smiles @ me membrane
sculpture that she is & tells
her creation myth how once
she was piled f/ the countless
sands of her a thousand
trembling sets & that s
the bottom lip alone *what*
a delicate rendering you are
I breathe

[View No. Two]

I was surprised to learn
she had no bones *silly*
she sways *you have*
no bones too I made her a pair
of bone shoes w/ points @
the toes & fractals to die for
colorless w/ glee *there s no*
such thing as bones she
curtsies

Some Views fl Thingèd Surface

[View No. Three]

I put her in my locket
where she tilts against
hydrangeas lovely season
for hydrangeas petals dilate
like silent operas they clot
their skeleton math when
I squint my locket s a mirror
& I look just like her not
to brag but I do *like a widen
ing pupil* she agrees *like
a wound*

[The Final View]

Behind her face lives a
chattering grid it taught me
how to navigate flickers
beneath her lid now I will
sail her vector dust past
curved whale spine &
back *funny goose* she laughs
there s nothing behind that

magus

Our father had in his repertoire
some really funny tricks. While mom

left to ready dessert, he'd regard us
from the distance of his

tipped-back chair, sing
Pick a hand—and whichever

one we'd choose
would bloom a wild black

cloud of ducks. When they made
my sister cry once, dad twirled

his sibylline mustache
and asked, *Did you know mallards*

nipped children's eyelids? Neither did I.

Like I said, these
powerful tricks could fill you with

true despair; there may be nothing
our dad can't do, because

a heedful set
—mother and sister and me—

you never will catch us
outdoors with no keys in our

pockets, so comes all the more
as a shock, how he

got us—our father—to lose him
completely, like magic, forget

him clean out of our world.

And, look, how it
breaks on deep-

fried pork rinds, on grease-smeared
fuchsia lips, now, at the deli—this

light: some dies
snail-like, retreats into an object's

private folds; some snarls back *Yes,*
a thing here (if you really

think it matters) for your
checklist of tragedies. But wait—that's

off: the Corner Tick Tock
Market-Lotto, a woman stopping

for cheesefries on her way home
from the club—

what, in all,
in any of these, could

be so unbearably grim? Only distortion
of surface, of tint—it's just a trick

of light, played by dad, wherever he is.

From his limitless life-
feats, though, could be the greatest

and most dismal's been
to strike each

trace, for him, of human
sympathy in us, so

we—who'd hardly managed
to cope with the natural

decline of our angelfish—can
with ease disregard

from the distance, as object
unnatural, our father: we've been

tricked into this—and with him
only, for all I know, a strange lonely

man, just a baffled old tragedy.

No News Today

No factories burn. No jets crash.
No natural disasters of epic proportions.
A man's pockets are not filling
with silver fish
and, above, there are no waves
hardly even a ripple.
A woman once again does not remember
to call the boiler repairman
who isn't chewing on a toothpick
beneath a bare lightbulb.
He does not hum the tune of a song from Les Miz
or stop as soon as he realizes he is doing it.
His name is not Robert.
No one is watching.
The playground no one uses,
rising from the trash-strewn weeds
and gravel behind Mickey Tires &
Auto Parts, is not a prehistoric
mastodon skeleton, where a lone swing
is not creaking your name
or anyone else's.
There are no runaways in the gazebo
and one, a debonair
redhead who, at fifteen,
can pass himself off as early twenties
did not just whisper something
into the ear of another—
a jittery, baby-faced girl, completely bald
under the oversize wool beanie she
never takes off—
causing her to let out
a quick, astonished laugh.

Nth Sunday in Ordinary Time

For a thousand years
we've lived here on this hissing rock.
Once I saw ankles

lift from the shallows.
The Ambassador, Dad told me
as we watched him wade

away. Bivalves, we gurgle,
we open and close.
When I wished

for a white sheet to drape us
when we're dead so it can rise
and fall in the breeze

from the fan, Ma
slapped me on the cheek.
When we're gone, the hole left

will be wider than life itself, she said.
Now, instead, I pray no
righteous match our

sputtered tail to
strike, meaning
the opposite of that:

it's an art we all learn.
When we leave there won't
be breeze and I won't have to miss

the whirr of the fan.
It is sad being
born to a punctured sphere;

but it's something
to hear stars at
night deflating slowly, slowly.

(Blessed Are) They Who Preserve

These glass jars are houses for little Human Acts.
Lavender Rhubard, its sticky architecture, its late-afternoon stipple: the work of
Mrs. Blackwell (who right
now is dicing yams). Look, such tidy
avenues she's paved across
her walls, it is a split
sea of jars, all
neatly named (Persimmon & Wild
Sumac Preserves, Candied Citron Pith, Green

Apple Ginger, Scuppernong, Cantaloupe, Grape). Ever since
her husband died, Mrs.
Blackwell (call her Mora) has
been afraid of flying, a disorder
named Aerophobia, says Dr. Ramirez—a real
shame because, this half-decade retired, Mora's French
has much improved (Noémie at Parlons Français! tells her often) & wouldn't it
be something else:
the trip, end of term,

to Toulouse. *Still*—she'll eye you in
confidence, under a framed sketch of a parsley sprig—*so*
much to fill the time: her Owlets (as she
calls the cats), her ceramic
sculpture class & in the evenings, who
would visit poor Lakshmi two floors up? Dear Lakshmi—like her, a widow, but
afraid of leaving home & chronic dyspnea &
her daughter, long
run off to Lord Knows Where.

Come, let us coo over each
other's maladies, in the light of
the lampshade, where (softly) knocks a fly.

Susanna coos—*Your little skin*—through the Lamp-
Rimmed Ultra Magnifying Glass—*Promise me no*
more you pick your
pretty your little
skin. Be careful not

to mention the vials she's stashed, free of charge, in your purse (Power Pore Vanishing
Daily Renewal Mist, Red Algae Face Polish, Wheat
Germ & Juniper Oil Avec Yuzu
Defense, Royal Fern Seed Time-Filler, Sage Perfect Purity Peel, Anti-

Aging Fig Leaf Mask) as the owner—Mr. M—has warned Susanna before, M-
Balm Beauty Solutions don't grow on trees & just between us don't you bet he'd can
her if not for her being so old? Old Susanna—one of two Einhorns of Szeged remaining ('All
this world's history is born of the races' instinct for self-preservation. All
not of good race in this world are chaff' & 'Cherish your perfect blood's own pureness! It
spells eternal life!' went the thinking back then). The other—Béla Einhorn: at work (a White
Castle, Queens) when in walks his Zsazsa, his own little
Zsuzsanna, after eight years & yet still—still alive. They married that same month (June,
1949) but afraid what the offspring of cousins would be—*My clients is my*

babies—she'll hunch over
the lamp-rimmed glass, stroking Sweet
Rose Root Milk on your cheek. (Let us coo.)

Over the 108 white minitiles of the bathroom floor, Paul
kneels—a weekly ritual since
leaving the Reverend his
father's home for this place above the Chick Shack ('FLAVORED
CHICKEN RINGS ARE ACK')—while, beside him, in a row, on a cloth
patterned with onion bulbs: the contents of the Immunotruth Kit he sent for in
the mail (Whole Blood Test Cassette, Desiccant Bag, Plastic Pipettes A & B, Developer
Fluid, Alcohol Pad, two Bandaids,
Lancet). Paul's mother used to lilt, a watched

pot never boils—& that one (at least) feels pretty
much on point even still, always careful not to check till the full
time's up, for the word on his fingerprick's issue. The others (Plainsight Diagnostics, Anti-
body Reveal, Orasure HIV 1 & 2, Rapid Serum-Seer, HemoGenuine, Avert,
Ora•cular) have so far always all come
out the same ('One line for Negative') the same result the same
faulty result because, really, how could they know—in the flesh—what he
has only himself
begun to detect

within him
what shadows (growing,
growing) of what unspeakable fruit.

Hush—
Mora will
clasp your hand
hard, when you say, well,
probably about time to get going, it's late. Then—*Yes*
yes yes, of course—she'll, smiling, gesture towards the special homemade jams & spreads
kept separate, as
gifts for her houseguests, on the shelf above
the coffee cups ('ASK MY WIFE' goes the writing on one, on another: 'W

for Wall! Spell a More Perfect Union! Preserve Our Nation!'
behind that, an eggshell
blue mug—'Ooh-la-la! C'est
magnifique!' with little Arc de Triomphes). & once the clink of your jars (Lazy Apricot, Plum) down
the block can no longer be heard from where (look) she is standing
so still—so perfectly, so unspeakably still—there on
her front screened-in porch right now, then
Mora—Mrs. Mora Blackwell—will

turn, lock
the door, dim the desk
lamp & softly (yes. Yes, softly) swat a fly.

III

III

Family Thanksgiving on Brimstone Island, Maine
(or, Apples to Oranges, Dust to Dust)

You bought the wrong kind of molasses. The mother is not mad, she has no needs or desires, she will make do. Is this for human consumption? There is no kinship term for the one who's talking about how this thing and also that thing, it seems to her, are different than before, because your brother's mother-in-law is of no relation to you. Is this for human consumption? No. Waves. Sand. Does something smell dead to anyone? These molasses are for cattle feed. The one who is talking says, It's like I've always said.

Formal Proof That the Universe Is Neither Cruel nor Kind, and That This Is the Greatest Conceivable Horror

1. An hour like this and the lobby is empty except for the clockwise-walkers. Just a scattering tonight, spinning wavily and lost-looking as ever in the room's outer edges. One of them keeps asking, though too softly to be heard, *Where is the person in charge?*

2. The redheaded child, firstborn male of the family from another, older country, has just seen a flea swoop from a dim, deep place on his cat, Dragomir, down, down into the even more dark rippling of his bedsheets.

3. Poor ancient Morty won't go to bed, not ever, without wandering through the whole building's corridors first. From wing to wing, the grasscloth walls he strokes and sighs.

4. Miss Suhn returns to find her home has been rented out to boarders. *Sure thing,* the handsome yolk-blond couple beams down from her open door. *It's on the far side of the half-moon console table along the hallway just to your left.* On the shelf above her toilet: a fake light-up fishtank.

5. Though complex, the laws of motion are real, very real, and etched on inviolable coils of invisible leaf. The whole ancient dilating seabed's other side is a single void-shaped tablet.

6. Louis shrieks, *Fish taco! You nasty—*

7. Once again, politely, the widow asks into the telephone receiver, *Yes, hello, yes now who is speaking please?* Around the Queen Anne chair's left arm is coiled a single long black sock.

8. *Forgot your keys again there, Morty?* croons the man with seagrass skin.

9. *Shut up, Louis,* interrupts everyone.

10. But when she wakes, everything in its order, its real order, and real: her bird's-eye quilt, her miniature jam jars. In the dark, Miss Suhn hears furniture being moved around upstairs.

11. From inside of him, or else from someplace closer, emptier, deeper: an ancient wail—so long, long, and horrible—a darkly dilating ripple. The horrible seaweed man repeats, *Forgot your keys again there, Morty?*

12. In a poster on a half-stripped wall, twelve bishops at an egg-shaped table encircling twelve egg cups. On each cup's porcelain surface is a scene depicting twelve bishops—the very same—around their porcelain egg cups, whose identical surfaces depict the above-mentioned scene.

13. The foreign boy counts under the blankets, while all around him everywhere beats to the black design of long-invisible strangers. Was there a word for that in his old language? This is the time when the sickle-wing nightjars, the whip-poor-wills might come.

14. *Please—who is speaking, who is this please, yes now who is there, who's there, who's there?* wife of the late Vice-Principal Wills paces, over and over, in infinitesimally beating circles bounded by the infinitesimally coiling telephone cord, cramped ripples traced in an ancient gyre, turning, turning, spinning, spun on an ancient axis, spinning rings around the ancient rotary dial round the dilating ancient void ringing, yes now ringing, ringing—and wrung.

5 Revelation Loop Apt 5L

The room upstairs is an
old woman with some mouth
singing *Trollop sky* when
the weather's clear *Your endless*
cunt offends Question

where d'you think she learned
that fancy shrillwork Opera school
Does black wallmold also appear to her
as poor lidless Saint Lucy When
the big tree's bare she laughs *You*

hack Whose void is
skulling now And
nighttime's when your ear
runs red with her scraped
lambsthroat howl Might

wonder don't her fingers
end at stunning gothic
tips Or isn't it funny how rooms
below don't seem to lodge
complaints regards the *Mangle me*

with currycombs pincers molten
lead curve my naked legs through
spokes cudgel my dustbin
head come at dark from
the sixth-floor walkup But

dawn her creak's so thin
must tease from the nextdoor
weedwacker's bluster with care
with love or all'd be lost her
creaky *Cut me down to many-*

embered flame becomes
my mind just no more

5 Revelation Loop Apt 5L

whites of your glass eye
please world don't cut
me down to size   Then

the stillest time of day   Also
the most important   This
is when she listens to me listening to
her listen to me   I
listen feeling skull inside my

face the walls grow blank

How Long Now Since the Mailman's Gone Missing?

It's a sad yellow feeling
like walking into someone else's childhood.

A flickering
inside a vast, black egg:

it's time to go.
The little shops pass

wall-less and candlelit
by night

and she (who greets you at the door)
her mouth

makes a warm cave.
The table's set

for dinner, dear. Yes.
No one

will unravel this (your home address) again.

Ileocecal

Their first date, she mentioned her friend, how she'd moved back home to Kathmandu. They were crunching on a soybean side dish called *musya palu*—at a Nepalese restaurant, that's why it came up. Wait, he wanted to know, these aren't peanuts. Peanuts got stuck inside his valve. I miss her badly though, she continued. We talk but we're so far apart. I like you, he said, and she looked down the dark behind his teeth, wondering about his valve, whose specific name, even as he'd pronounced it, had sounded unpronounceably foreign. It isn't *mine*, he'd kept trying to explain. This valve is in you, too. After dinner, they walked down the pulsing tunnel of tree shadows faulty streetlights billboard silhouettes—then they were there, and she knew he'd be coming inside. Well, she sang, here we are. Home sweet home.

I Am the Perennial Head of This One-person Subcutaneous Wrecking Crew

To maintain these depths of misery
takes work given my buoyant disposition;
for every sill of my flesh
I must invent a new method to flay.
Few people know inside your skin

is a microscopic garden.
With love I tuck in seeds
of its destruction late
each night, daily tend my

dear ruin—knot distant, unsuspecting
clovers at their root tips; stomata full of
rodent bones, down

they go, the pond lilies: I'm strict. Who
could love you like you.

Conversations with Death

I bit my tongue
Don't forget

Your umbrella. At
The fair. *Spit it*

Out. Ventoso &
Vamp was in town that day only a

Few hours more. Please. *What*
Yes? What? No

Nothing. Just
A large buttered popcorn

I chewed
Too fast. Pain then. It

Came as a shock. *Did it ever*
Stop? Bright

Dots. Slip-
Pery buttons. Yes I

Remember my favorite shirt
On the collar how sudden black

Blood. No it's never
Come out. *But here we*

Are. Ready? Step
Right up. Hot

And fresh. A full
Bucket that's wide as your

Face. Yesiree just one ace to
Peep inside

The furious whirling glass
Cocoon's closed

Circuit of perfect
Fleecy white explosions

Sylphic bursting open
Kernels plunging

Headlong endlessly
Looked just like my inklings

Then of what
Love must be. *So*

So now love
I know

Is the husk
Caught and throbbing under

Your gums. *So*
That's it? Wait

I hardly even got a chance yet
To begin. Still haven't

Ridden the Mad Sheikh's
Final Word or

Felt the world's thorniest
Dwarf or played

Quicken the
Chicken before

The hot hand led me
Home. Spit it out

Mother said so
The sylph fell

Stained and crumpled in
Her palm from my raveling

Mouth. Although how did she
She must have

Found me. She
Must have heard

Me. I must
Have cried. I was young. I split

My tongue. There was blood. I'm
Sorry. It just came as

A shock and well she knew
Me so completely I even could

Let her finish my thought
But I never meant

I mean I didn't
Ever want to be

Put to bed while
The sun and wild slippery

Squawks of mad ballyhoo-talkers
Still caught in

The curtains. Blustery
Morning. Don't

Forget your umbrella she called
But I did. Didn't

Matter. Right
Back again soon

And no wind
No there never

Has ever been any wind there's no
Wind in this room. *Listen—it's*

Time to leave. Yes hear
That whistling old

Calliope? Play! Play higher now
Louder closer—please. Closer. I

Would let her finish
Even my thought

The way she would pick
Green apples from the branch

Then eat one
Wearing plastic gloves

The right hand led it to her lips
And in the left

With every bite
She spit

The chewed-up little skins. *Who's*
This? Your mother? You're

Raving again. Wrong
It was you I meant

You all along. *Good*
Yes. Good. Vent. Get these things

Off your chest. I see. Draw me out
Headlong then

Lap me
To rest. I've

Always been chicken
And crumpled in

A dumb husk
Always been caught always

Throbbed away
Speechlessly under

The sheets
While somewhere so close maybe

Outside my
Window I needed to go

To where
Was it

And something
Important I've always been trying to say

Yes? Well? Sure
Gloomy this

Weather. I have
My umbrella. Windless

Though. Strange. Too fast
Too fast too—How

Sudden black. Don't
you remember? *Spit*

It out. Someone
Has picked

My pocket. Look—my bright
Nickels all got spent. *Time's up.* But

Oh but I had meant
To buy us

Both chewing-
Gum cigarettes. *Come*

Out. Wait. Can
You recollect

A thing that
Hasn't happened yet? *Come.* Yes? *Come*

Yes I *forget.*

In the Valley of the Choice Vine II: The Wax Museum

We are all of us, silently, approaching the fixed point. Every time I think this, the same music—instrumentals from a movie sequel I'll come close to seeing but will never see—plays in one of my brain's shuttered rooms.

Some of it was told to me by a locksmith with glass eyes. Nine months before discovering her rare blood disease, a girl will ask me to the local cinema, a rust-tinted uniplex stalled at 1959. The movie will have premiered that weekend to wide acclaim; in her front-page review, an influential critic will have used words like *surprising* and *propulsive*.

I will love everything about the girl: her strangely hairless umbilical region; how she'll fix on your mouth as it speaks with her stare, her stare fixed in its state of unbounded unblinking. But an hour before our date, I'll text *must take rain check sadly so sry*, a lie about a great-uncle Samson who doesn't exist. I'll stop returning the girl's calls but will save each voicemail she leaves in my voicemail inbox.

When the couple nextdoor moves uptown, I'll move to their true one-bedroom-plus-den. It will be railroad-style but bigger than my current apartment; the kitchen will get better light. I live above a wax museum that—though the sign on the door says *Open 9 AM to 5 PM every Tues to Sun!*—I have yet to witness anybody enter, still, or exit.

Penance

I offer up
this flowerbox my skull

dear whoever
let its luxuriance

exceed its baseness
let me curl

in the blueblack
root hairs and wait

for you
wind in my teeth

will sough sweetly

Arpeggio Progression in Missing Key

1

& look we're on a raft
in the sun on a raft really getting
somewhere now   I got kelp
on my leg
on the swim over

2

do you asks pretty
sue *know what*

I love what pretty
please tell us

3

leeches on my shin
might have been

barnacles maybe the point is

that it's gone now
or it might have been algae

4

one two three
here we

are and before we know
it we are still here look

in the sun the clanging
sun listen

it's counting

5

do you asks pretty

sue *know what*

I love pretty

please tell us tell us

what we give up

6

I knew

a boy once

I liked the

funny way

that he

said *satan*

7

on the way to where
we're going

Arpeggio Progression in Missing Key

we talk about missing

things on dry land on dry land
someone had a heavenly
peacock they never took out

of the box the box
said its function was changing
direction immediately when hitting
obstacles
& flashing

the peacock will give you infinite
pleasure its neck can
stagger it is
feather consecutive who knows

if any of that's true though it was all
according to the box

8

what's that
over there

is it
slickening whales

is it
quickening
kelp lit by sun no that's

just us upon the face of the waters we look

so watery
thin & countless that I've lost
                                        count did

you notice

9

do you know what
I love no one

two three
we give

up *that you can never get*

too tan oh true

for sue is more ravishing

than a headful of hazard than flame than sideways
lawnchairs in an ocean of wheat she is wheat to

us she is
an amber onslaught

10

I am on a raft who

are you are you

on a raft too

then we must be

like two

black piano keys

are we

near one another

I wonder how

I wish

one day we'd touch

11

someone misses
wheat someone

misses lawnchairs

but we are better than that we
say we are better
than lawnchairs strewn sideways &
the drouthy grass beneath where a little egg
salad still nestles from

the party your grandma
is drinking too much gin and the children
glide into the bushes where

did everyone go

12

on the way
there *it changed*
direction someone says *upon*

hitting obstacles
my peacock why
we ask

are you hitting yourself are
you hitting yourself
are you

13

on the way to
where we are

talking about

missing things on the
way to where

we're

            missing things

14

on the way to where we're
going

someone tells a funny joke

about a family
of flies a family of flies walks into

my ear

nobody home they say
& leave

15

oh hello yes hello yes yoo hoo
yes it's us over here yes it's true

we've made great strides
you must not recognize

it's just us yes long way though we've come
yes our pretty sue will be so tan soon you'll
confuse her with the sun

16

do you know about
my love

the way he said *satan*

it rhymed
          with *plankton*

17

we are on a raft
a real raft on a
raft really getting
somewhere now   I got krill
on my self on

the swim
here but it's gone now

18

& look sue is more beautiful
than tuna

on wheat or eggless
egg salad than endless

sandwiches in the shade
than a sandswept palace no one has
lived in for
years or whales strewn
staggered

on long
lonely sand

19

but then *what*

do you miss asks
everyone & pretty sue
is listening too though

none of us can hear
above the clanging no

wind no waves like everything
we left
behind my answer still

hangs there

one more
vapor
thin   peep in the air

under the sun's
swelling thumb

A Note About the Author

Danielle Blau's *Rhyme or Reason: Poets and Philosophers on the Problem of Being Here Now* is forthcoming from W. W. Norton. Her collection *mere eye* was selected for a Poetry Society of America Chapbook Award and published with an introduction by D. A. Powell, and her poems won first place in the multi-genre *Narrative* 30 Below Contest. Poetry, short stories, articles, and interviews by Blau appear in *The Atlantic*, *Australian Book Review*, *The Baffler*, *The Literary Review*, *Narrative Magazine*, *The New Yorker*'s book blog, *The Paris Review*, *Ploughshares*, *The Saint Ann's Review*, several volumes of the *Plume Anthology of Poetry*, and elsewhere. Her work has been set to music by composers of various stripes and performed in such venues as Museum of Contemporary Art Australia and Carnegie Hall. A graduate of Brown University with an honors degree in philosophy, and of New York University with an MFA in poetry, she curates and hosts the monthly Gavagai Music + Reading Series in Brooklyn, teaches at Hunter College in Manhattan, and lives with her son Kai in Queens.

A Note About the Anthony Hecht Poetry Prize

The Anthony Hecht Poetry Prize was inaugurated in 2005 and is awarded on an annual basis to the best first or second collection of poems submitted.

First Annual Hecht Prize
Judge: J. D. McClatchy
Winner: Morri Creech, *Field Knowledge*

Second Annual Hecht Prize
Judge: Mary Jo Salter
Winner: Erica Dawson, *Big-Eyed Afraid*

Third Annual Hecht Prize
Judge: Richard Wilbur
Winner: Rose Kelleher, *Bundle o' Tinder*

Fourth Annual Hecht Prize
Judge: Alan Shapiro
Winner: Carrie Jerrell, *After the Revival*

Fifth Annual Hecht Prize
Judge: Rosanna Warren
Winner: Matthew Ladd, *The Book of Emblems*

Sixth Annual Hecht Prize
Judge: James Fenton
Winner: Mark Kraushaar, *The Uncertainty Principle*

Seventh Annual Hecht Prize
Judge: Mark Strand
Winner: Chris Andrews, *Lime Green Chair*

Eighth Annual Hecht Prize
Judge: Charles Simic
Winner: Shelley Puhak, *Guinevere in Baltimore*

Ninth Annual Hecht Prize
Judge: Heather McHugh
Winner: Geoffrey Brock, *Voices Bright Flags*

Tenth Annual Hecht Prize
Judge: Anthony Thwaite
Winner: Jaimee Hills, *How to Avoid Speaking*

Eleventh Annual Hecht Prize
Judge: Eavan Boland
Winner: Austin Allen, *Pleasures of the Game*

Twelfth Annual Hecht Prize
Judge: Gjertrud Schnackenberg
Winner: Mike White, *Addendum to a Miracle*

Thirteenth Annual Hecht Prize
Judge: Andrew Motion
Winner: Christopher Cessac, *The Youngest Ocean*

Fourteenth Annual Hecht Prize
Judge: Charles Wright
Winner: Katherine Hollander, *My German Dictionary*

Fifteenth Annual Hecht Prize
Judge: Edward Hirsch
Winner: James Davis, *Club Q*

Sixteenth Annual Hecht Prize
Judge: Vijay Seshadri
Winner: Danielle Blau, *peep*

Other Books from Waywiser

Poetry

Austin Allen, *Pleasures of the Game*
Al Alvarez, *New & Selected Poems*
Chris Andrews, *Lime Green Chair*
Audrey Bohanan, *Any Keep or Contour*
George Bradley, *A Few of Her Secrets*
Geoffrey Brock, *Voices Bright Flags*
Christopher Cessac, *The Youngest Ocean*
Robert Conquest, *Blokelore & Blokesongs*
Robert Conquest, *Collected Poems*
Robert Conquest, *Penultimata*
Morri Creech, *Blue Rooms*
Morri Creech, *Field Knowledge*
Morri Creech, *The Sleep of Reason*
Peter Dale, *One Another*
James Davis, *Club Q*
Erica Dawson, *Big-Eyed Afraid*
B. H. Fairchild, *The Art of the Lathe*
David Ferry, *On This Side of the River: Selected Poems*
Daniel Groves & Greg Williamson, eds., *Jiggery-Pokery Semicentennial*
Jeffrey Harrison, *The Names of Things: New & Selected Poems*
Joseph Harrison, *Identity Theft*
Joseph Harrison, *Shakespeare's Horse*
Joseph Harrison, *Someone Else's Name*
Joseph Harrison, *Sometimes I Dream That I Am Not Walt Whitman*
Joseph Harrison, ed., *The Hecht Prize Anthology, 2005-2009*
Anthony Hecht, *Collected Later Poems*
Anthony Hecht, *The Darkness and the Light*
Jaimee Hills, *How to Avoid Speaking*
Katherine Hollander, *My German Dictionary*
Hilary S. Jacqmin, *Missing Persons*
Carrie Jerrell, *After the Revival*
Stephen Kampa, *Articulate as Rain*
Stephen Kampa, *Bachelor Pad*
Rose Kelleher, *Bundle o' Tinder*
Mark Kraushaar, *The Uncertainty Principle*
Matthew Ladd, *The Book of Emblems*
J. D. McClatchy, *Plundered Hearts: New and Selected Poems*
Dora Malech, *Shore Ordered Ocean*
Jérôme Luc Martin, *The Gardening Fires: Sonnets and Fragments*
Eric McHenry, *Odd Evening*
Eric McHenry, *Potscrubber Lullabies*
Eric McHenry and Nicholas Garland, *Mommy Daddy Evan Sage*
Eugenio Montale: *Late Montale: Poems Written in His Final Years, Selected and Translated by George Bradley*
Timothy Murphy, *Very Far North*
Ian Parks, *Shell Island*
V. Penelope Pelizzon, *Whose Flesh is Flame, Whose Bone is Time*
Chris Preddle, *Cattle Console Him*
Shelley Puhak, *Guinevere in Baltimore*
Christopher Ricks, ed., *Joining Music with Reason: 34 Poets, British and American, Oxford 2004-2009*
Daniel Rifenburgh, *Advent*
Mary Jo Salter, *It's Hard to Say: Selected Poems*
W. D. Snodgrass, *Not for Specialists: New & Selected Poems*

Other Books from Waywiser

Mark Strand, *Almost Invisible*
Mark Strand, *Blizzard of One*
Bradford Gray Telford, *Perfect Hurt*
Matthew Thorburn, *This Time Tomorrow*
Cody Walker, *Shuffle and Breakdown*
Cody Walker, *The Self-Styled No-Child*
Cody Walker, *The Trumpiad*
Deborah Warren, *The Size of Happiness*
Clive Watkins, *Already the Flames*
Clive Watkins, *Jigsaw*
Richard Wilbur, *Anterooms*
Richard Wilbur, *Mayflies*
Richard Wilbur, *Collected Poems 1943-2004*
Norman Williams, *One Unblinking Eye*
Greg Williamson, *A Most Marvelous Piece of Luck*
Greg Williamson, *The Hole Story of Kirby the Sneak and Arlo the True*
Stephen Yenser, *Stone Fruit*

Fiction

Gregory Heath, *The Entire Animal*
Mary Elizabeth Pope, *Divining Venus*
K. M. Ross, *The Blinding Walk*
Gabriel Roth, *The Unknowns**
Matthew Yorke, *Chancing It*

Illustrated

Nicholas Garland, *I wish ...*
Eric McHenry and Nicholas Garland, *Mommy Daddy Evan Sage*
Greg Williamson, *The Hole Story of Kirby the Sneak and Arlo the True*

Non-Fiction

Neil Berry, *Articles of Faith: The Story of British Intellectual Journalism*
Irving Feldman, *Usable Truths: Aphorisms & Observations*
Mark Ford, *A Driftwood Altar: Essays and Reviews*
Philip Hoy, ed., *A Bountiful Harvest: The Correspondence of Anthony Hecht and William L. MacDonald*
John Rosenthal, *Searching for Amylu Danzer*
Richard Wollheim, *Germs: A Memoir of Childhood*

*Co-published with Picador